The
NON-ALCOHOLIC
COCKTAIL
BOOK

The
NON-ALCOHOLIC
COCKTAIL
BOOK

David Bevan

Ebury Press
London

Planned and produced by Tigerlily Ltd
Illustrated by Nicola Spoor
Designed by Anthony Lawrence &
Hilly Beavan

Published By Ebury Press
Division of The National Magazine Company Ltd
Colquhoun House
27–37 Broadwick Street
London W1V 1FR

First impression 1986

ISBN 0 85223 432 5

Computerset in Great Britain by MFK Typesetting Ltd., Hitchin,
Hertfordshire

Printed and bound in Yugoslavia by Mladinska knjiga,
Ljubljana

·CONTENTS·

6

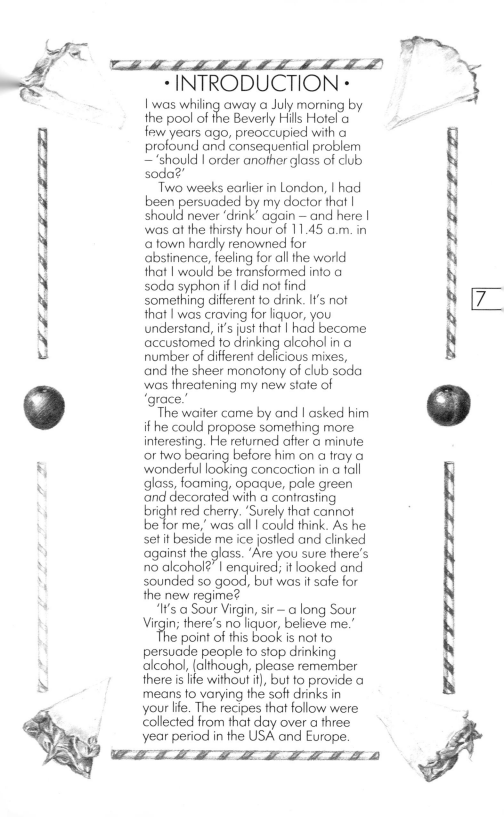

· INTRODUCTION ·

I was whiling away a July morning by the pool of the Beverly Hills Hotel a few years ago, preoccupied with a profound and consequential problem — 'should I order *another* glass of club soda?'

Two weeks earlier in London, I had been persuaded by my doctor that I should never 'drink' again — and here I was at the thirsty hour of 11.45 a.m. in a town hardly renowned for abstinence, feeling for all the world that I would be transformed into a soda syphon if I did not find something different to drink. It's not that I was craving for liquor, you understand, it's just that I had become accustomed to drinking alcohol in a number of different delicious mixes, and the sheer monotony of club soda was threatening my new state of 'grace.'

The waiter came by and I asked him if he could propose something more interesting. He returned after a minute or two bearing before him on a tray a wonderful looking concoction in a tall glass, foaming, opaque, pale green *and* decorated with a contrasting bright red cherry. 'Surely that cannot be for me,' was all I could think. As he set it beside me ice jostled and clinked against the glass. 'Are you sure there's no alcohol?' I enquired; it looked and sounded so good, but was it safe for the new regime?

'It's a Sour Virgin, sir — a long Sour Virgin; there's no liquor, believe me.'

The point of this book is not to persuade people to stop drinking alcohol, (although, please remember there is life without it), but to provide a means to varying the soft drinks in your life. The recipes that follow were collected from that day over a three year period in the USA and Europe.

· THE ESSENTIALS ·

Most of the soft-drink ingredients in this book are widely available but if you decide you want to embark on the more esoteric and unusual drinks you may need a root vegetable juicer. Equally you could probably use most of the attachments for a kitchen blender if you plan to use fresh ingredients, such as may be allowed by considerations of time and season. I suggest, otherwise, that you can survive with just a blender, a fruit squeezer, a cocktail shaker and a large glass jug.

GLASSES
Of course you do not need special glasses for these drinks, but you will enjoy using a range of glasses if they are available. I think of three types of glass that a bartender would use for long drinks or cocktails.

The Cocktail Glass – normally on a stem and with very little capacity – this type of glass is for delicate drinks or guests.

The Highball Glass. A tall straight sided tumbler which holds about 300 ml (½ pint).

The Old Fashioned Glass. Straight sided, but smaller than the Highball, this will hold 150–200 ml (¼–⅓ pint). Suitable for straight or slightly diluted drinks.

MIXERS AND SYRUPS
In addition to all the fresh fruit drinks I have given, there is another world altogether in combining the various prepared 'mixers', cordials and syrups.

I will suggest a few of my personal favourites and you will get the idea:

Orange squash or lemon squash diluted with ginger beer rather than tap water.

Grenadine syrup in tonic water with lots of ice and a twist of lemon.

Cassis syrup in bitter lemon garnished as above.

There are a number of ready prepared syrups available from good stores. The range French/English consists of:

Anis	Aniseed
Cassis	Blackcurrant
Citron	Lemon
Fraise	Strawberry
Framboise	Raspberry
Gomme	Sugar Syrup/Rock Candy
Grenadine	Pomegranate
Grosseille	Redcurrant
Menthe	Mint
Orange	Orange
Orgeat	Almond

Gomme is about the only one which does not make a good drink simply diluted – but you will notice it is used frequently as a sweetener. You may substitute its use for sugar where indicated according to whether you want a gritty texture in your drink, which is sometimes rather interesting.

All the others make delicious drinks mixed individually with tonic or bitter lemon. Children of all ages will be very impressed with the colours.

A NOTE ON THE RECIPES
In some cases, mainly where simple, I have indicated the proportions by which the

constituents should be added to whatever glass or container you intend to use. In others where the process is more complicated I have given servings for 2–10. In either case, in the event of a party, soft drinks look enticing in large glass jugs and standing for short periods prior to serving enhances the reaction of flavours on each other.

Generally speaking the recipes are grouped together according to the principal ingredient. If you wish to find out all the recipes in the book which use any one ingredient, however, you should consult the Index.

SPARKLING WATER
Sparkling water means whatever you prefer out of club soda/soda water/mineral water to dilute and effervesce your drinks. I use Perrier water myself as I have found that it is taste-free, holds it's bubbles well and is widely available; but anything meeting the first two criteria is fine. You should avoid mineral waters with heavy mineral contents as these do frightful things to the flavour.

CHILDREN
Children love brightly coloured drinks – generally avoid the *Let's Pretend* section when catering to children only, as these drinks have sharp/sour tastes. Use syrups liberally and make familiar tastes and unusual colours, or food colourings – to turn lemonade blue for example.

· PRESENTATION ·

Think of your soft drinks like you think of hard ones and embellish them a little – not every Orange Sling needs a harvest festival of *glacé* fruits impaled on a miniature umbrella, but you can try one of the following decorative suggestions for suitable occasions.

CHILL
Chill your glasses in the freezer for ten minutes or so before use. The drink you serve will cause condensation to form on the glass – an attractive effect used in advertising material for many brands of gin and vodka to entice you.

Warning. Do not chill crystal – it shatters; and over-zealous chilling is anti-social.

OR DIP
Sugar – or salt: dip the rims of the glasses. This is both attractive and delicious. Prepare a plate of ground white sugar or salt according to the drinks you are serving. Moisten the rim and top 1 cm (½ in) of each glass with lemon or lime juice. Invert glasses into the powder, sugar or salt. The powder will stick to the juice and set like a frost on the top of each glass.

REMEMBER THE ICE
Add plenty of ice to all drinks for decoration and aural satisfaction. It is very unrewarding to be toying with an uniced silent vase of grapefruit or whatever during a lull in conversation. Ice makes a drink sound like a drink.

DO NOT FORGET THE CHERRY

·ORCHARD FRUITS·

·CITRUS BLISS·

Thanks to John Shelley of the East Hampton Volleyball team for this favoured beach thirst quencher.

Juice of ½ lime
Juice of ½ lemon
¼ orange juice
¼ grapefruit juice
½ sparkling water
Mint (optional)

Mix the juices in a tall glass or jug with plenty of cracked ice. Dilute with chilled sparkling water. Decorate with fresh mint.

· CINDERELLA ·

⅓ orange juice
⅓ lemon juice
⅓ pineapple juice

Shake together over ice and strain
into chilled cocktail glasses.

· MINTED ORANGE ·

1 pint orange juice
2½ fl oz lime juice
2 oz sugar
10 stems of fresh mint
Sparkling water

Rinse and strip the mint leaves from
the stems. Bring slowly to the boil
half the orange juice, sugar and
mint leaves; remove from the heat
and allow to cool for an hour or
two. Pour into a jug and add the
remaining orange juice and lime
juice and chill. To serve: pour over
ice and fill glasses ½–⅔ and top
up with chilled sparkling water.
Serves 3–4.

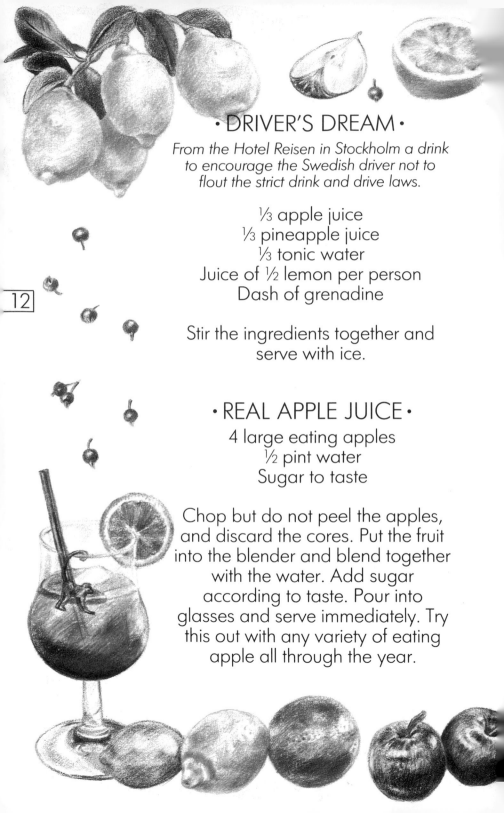

· DRIVER'S DREAM ·

*From the Hotel Reisen in Stockholm a drink
to encourage the Swedish driver not to
flout the strict drink and drive laws.*

⅓ apple juice
⅓ pineapple juice
⅓ tonic water
Juice of ½ lemon per person
Dash of grenadine

Stir the ingredients together and
serve with ice.

· REAL APPLE JUICE ·

4 large eating apples
½ pint water
Sugar to taste

Chop but do not peel the apples,
and discard the cores. Put the fruit
into the blender and blend together
with the water. Add sugar
according to taste. Pour into
glasses and serve immediately. Try
this out with any variety of eating
apple all through the year.

· REAL LEMONADE ·

6 fresh lemons
4 oz sugar
1¾ pints water

Wash the lemons, and peel the
rinds into a bowl with the sugar
and 1 litre of boiling water. Cover
the bowl and leave until cool.
Strain the mixture into a tall glass
jug, and add the juice of the lemon
fruit. Chill thoroughly and serve
with slices of lemon or lime and
mint leaves. Serves 6–8.

13

· PEACH AND ORANGE COCKTAIL ·

⅓ peach juice
⅓ orange juice
⅓ sparkling water

Stir together the juices over ice, and
add the chilled sparkling water. Stir
again and decorate with a cherry
and a slice of orange.

· GINGER PEACH ·

2 large peaches
2 oz sugar
Juice of 1 small orange or
tangerine
¼ tsp powdered ginger
Juice of 1 lemon
Ginger beer

Pare and stone the peaches, chop them coarsely and blend to a purée with sugar, juices and seasoning. Refrigerate for 30 minutes. Serve in tall glasses over cracked ice diluted with equal amount of ginger beer. Serves 2.

· SAVOY SPORTSMAN ·

Juice of 1 lemon
Juice of 1 lime
1 tsp grenadine
Tonic water

Pour the juices and grenadine into
a tumbler over cracked ice. Fill up
the glass with tonic water and stir
together. Decorate with a slice of
lemon.

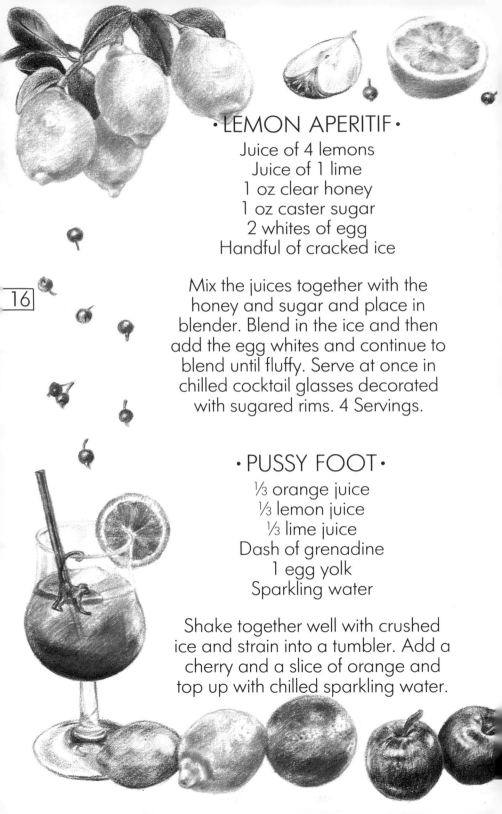

·LEMON APERITIF·

Juice of 4 lemons
Juice of 1 lime
1 oz clear honey
1 oz caster sugar
2 whites of egg
Handful of cracked ice

Mix the juices together with the
honey and sugar and place in
blender. Blend in the ice and then
add the egg whites and continue to
blend until fluffy. Serve at once in
chilled cocktail glasses decorated
with sugared rims. 4 Servings.

·PUSSY FOOT·

⅓ orange juice
⅓ lemon juice
⅓ lime juice
Dash of grenadine
1 egg yolk
Sparkling water

Shake together well with crushed
ice and strain into a tumbler. Add a
cherry and a slice of orange and
top up with chilled sparkling water.

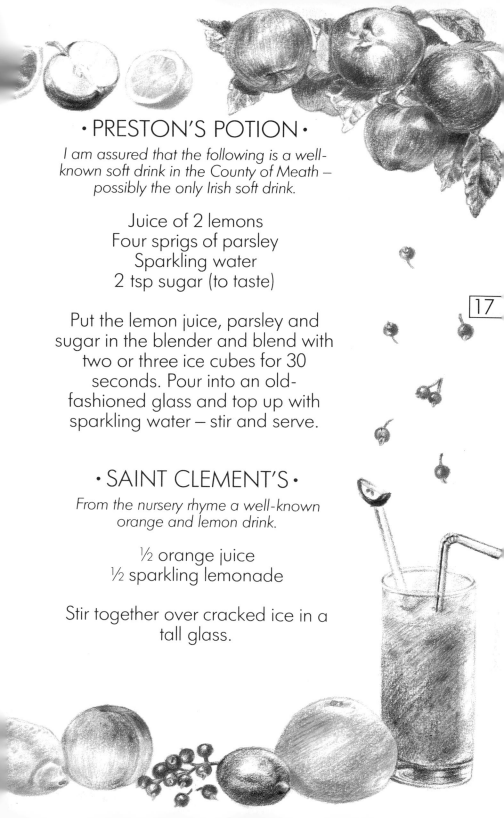

· PRESTON'S POTION ·

I am assured that the following is a well-known soft drink in the County of Meath — possibly the only Irish soft drink.

Juice of 2 lemons
Four sprigs of parsley
Sparkling water
2 tsp sugar (to taste)

Put the lemon juice, parsley and sugar in the blender and blend with two or three ice cubes for 30 seconds. Pour into an old-fashioned glass and top up with sparkling water — stir and serve.

· SAINT CLEMENT'S ·

From the nursery rhyme a well-known orange and lemon drink.

½ orange juice
½ sparkling lemonade

Stir together over cracked ice in a tall glass.

· SPORTSMAN ·

½ orange juice
¼ lemon juice
Dash of grenadine
¼ sparkling water
Fresh mint (optional)

Serve over ice stirring ingredients together. Decorate with fresh mint stalk.

· RASPBERRY AND LEMONADE ·

Juice of 2 lemons
1 fl oz raspberry syrup
Sparkling water

Put the lemon juice, syrup and ice in a blender and blend for 15 seconds. Pour into a highball glass and top up with sparkling water. Decorate with a twist of lemon peel.

· VERY BITTER LEMON ·

6 whole lemons
1 pint water
2 oz sugar
Sparkling water

Wash the fruit and cut it into pieces.
Place the fruit in a saucepan and
cover with the water. Bring to the
boil, cover and simmer for 15
minutes or so, by which time the
fruit will be soft. Stir in the sugar,
remove from the heat and leave
until cool. Strain into a glass jug
and refrigerate before serving.
Serve decorated with fresh sprigs
of mint over ice and dilute roughly
equally with sparkling water.
Serves 4.

· THIRST AID ·

2/8 fresh lime juice
1/8 blackcurrant juice
5/8 sparkling water

Pour ingredients into a highball
glass with plenty of ice and stir
together.

·PARSON'S DOSE·

⅙ grenadine
⅚ orange juice
1 egg yolk

Shake together well over cracked
ice and strain into chilled glass.

· REAL LEMON BARLEY WATER ·

A traditional and long established cooling drink, close your eyes and you're back in the days of the Raj.

Rind and juice of 4 lemons
4 pints water
2 oz pearl barley
1½ oz sugar

Rinse and bring the barley to a boil over a low heat. Stir the sugar and the juice and rind of lemon little by little into the boiling barley water. Withdraw container from heat, cover and leave to cool for six hours or so. Strain into a jug and chill well before serving.
Serves 6–8.

·VEGETABLES AND BERRIES·

·REAL TOMATO JUICE·

4 large tomatoes
¼ pint water
1 tsp sugar
Salt
Tabasco and Worcester sauce
(optional)
Juice of 1 lemon (optional)

Peel the tomatoes and put them in a blender with the remainder of the ingredients. Blend thoroughly and serve immediately over lots of ice. The addition of the juice of one lemon and some Tabasco and Worcester sauce to taste will get you another version of a *'Pure'* Mary. Serves 2–3.

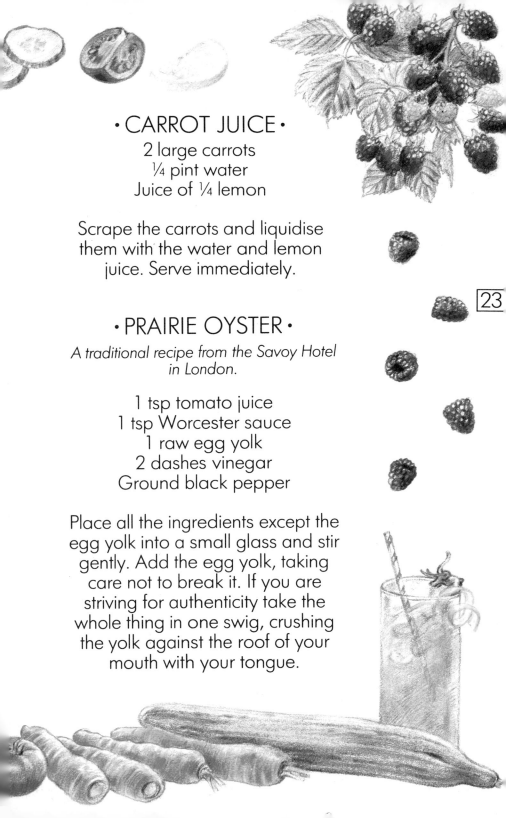

· CARROT JUICE ·

2 large carrots
¼ pint water
Juice of ¼ lemon

Scrape the carrots and liquidise
them with the water and lemon
juice. Serve immediately.

· PRAIRIE OYSTER ·

*A traditional recipe from the Savoy Hotel
in London.*

1 tsp tomato juice
1 tsp Worcester sauce
1 raw egg yolk
2 dashes vinegar
Ground black pepper

Place all the ingredients except the
egg yolk into a small glass and stir
gently. Add the egg yolk, taking
care not to break it. If you are
striving for authenticity take the
whole thing in one swig, crushing
the yolk against the roof of your
mouth with your tongue.

· GRAPE DELIGHT ·

1 pint grape juice
1 pint apple juice
Juice of 2 lemons
¼ pint *Sirop de Gomme*/rock candy
6 oz peeled and pitted grapes
1 small banana
1 litre bottle sparkling water

Chill the fruit juices and sparkling water separately in a refrigerator. Put the lemon juice and sugar syrup together and chill. When ready to serve mix the fruit juices and syrup in a large jug, serve over cracked ice in long glasses 'together' with grape and banana slivers, use ¾ mixture to ¼ sparkling water. Stir again once poured and add a slice of lemon.
Serves 10.

24

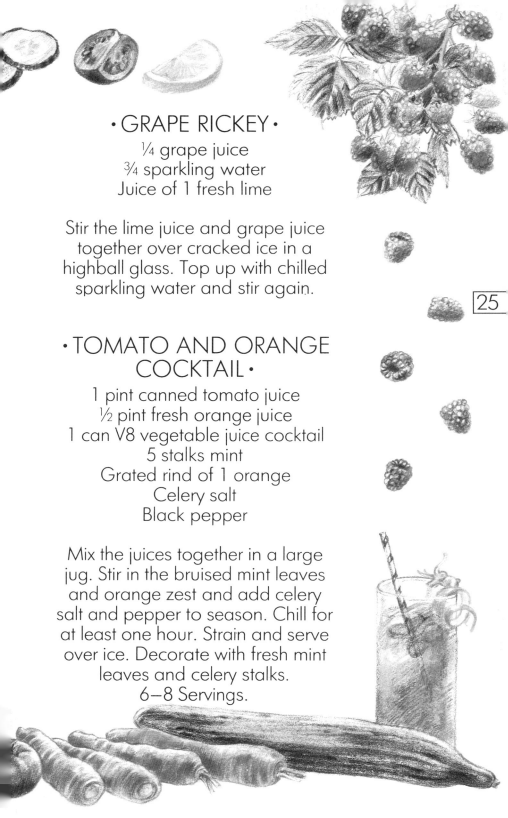

· GRAPE RICKEY ·

¼ grape juice
¾ sparkling water
Juice of 1 fresh lime

Stir the lime juice and grape juice
together over cracked ice in a
highball glass. Top up with chilled
sparkling water and stir again.

· TOMATO AND ORANGE COCKTAIL ·

1 pint canned tomato juice
½ pint fresh orange juice
1 can V8 vegetable juice cocktail
5 stalks mint
Grated rind of 1 orange
Celery salt
Black pepper

Mix the juices together in a large
jug. Stir in the bruised mint leaves
and orange zest and add celery
salt and pepper to season. Chill for
at least one hour. Strain and serve
over ice. Decorate with fresh mint
leaves and celery stalks.
6–8 Servings.

• COFFE TEA OR MILK •

• CHOCOLATE MINT •

½ chilled milk
½ vanilla ice cream
Green food colouring
Flaked or grated chocolate
Peppermint essence

Blend together in the blender the milk, ice cream and four or five drops per person of peppermint essence. When smooth add a few drops of the green colouring to give a good ghoulish hue. Pour into long glasses and decorate lavishly with grated or flaked chocolate.

· VIENNA VELVET ·

From the Sacher Hotel in Vienna where chocolate and coffee combinations are prolific.

For each serving
Chocolate ice cream
Double strength large measure of hot Espresso coffee
Lightly whipped cream

Fill two thirds of the serving glass with chocolate ice cream. Pour over it the hot coffee, and top with lashings of whipped cream.

· PEPPERMINT CHOCOLATE CREAM ·

1 glass hot milk
3 tsp drinking chocolate powder
5 peppermint creams

Put all the ingredients together in a blender and blend for 20 seconds. Serve immediately in mug or long hot-drink glass.

· CHOCOLATE MALTED MILK ·

The malted recipes, as you will observe, are fairly similar except for the flavourings. You can try your own variation of flavours either by blending together the appropriate sauce and ice cream, or by using the vanilla malted recipe as a base – leave aside the vanilla sauce and substitute a fruit sauce or even fresh fruit flesh. On this basis I can particularly recommend nectarines – use 1 ripe fruit per person.

½ pint chilled milk
1 heaped tbsp malted milk
3 large scoops chocolate ice cream
3 tbsp chocolate sauce

Place these ingredients together in a blender and blend for 30–45 seconds until smooth. Serve immediately. Serves two adults or one child.

· STRAWBERRY MALTED MILK ·

½ pint chilled milk
1 heaped tbsp malted milk
3 large scoops strawberry ice cream
2 tbsp strawberry sauce

Place all these ingredients in a blender and blend for 30–45 seconds until smooth. Serve immediately. Serves two adults or one child.

· VANILLA MALTED ·

½ pint chilled milk
1 heaped tbsp malted milk
3 large scoops vanilla ice cream
4 tbsp vanilla syrup

Put all these ingredients into a blender and blend for 30–45 seconds. Serve immediately. Serves two adults or one child.

• VANILLA MILKSHAKE •

For each serving blend together equal amounts of
Chilled milk
Vanilla ice cream
¼ tsp vanilla essence

Place these ingredients in a blender and blend for 30 seconds or so until smooth and creamy. Serve immediately in a tall glass, with a straw. To make a chocolate milkshake, replace vanilla essence with 1 tbsp chocolate sauce.

• BANANA MILKSHAKE •

1 peeled banana
½ vanilla ice cream
½ chilled milk
2 tsp brown sugar

Place the ingredients in a blender and blend for 30 seconds until smooth. Serve in a long glass immediately.

· STRAWBERRY MILK SHAKE ·

For each serving blend together
8 oz fresh washed and hulled
strawberries
2 large scoops vanilla ice cream

Liquidise the fruit first and then add
the ice cream and blend until
smooth. Serve immediately.

· ORANGE MILKSHAKE ·

For each person
½ vanilla ice cream
½ orange juice
1–2 oz dried skimmed milk
1 egg

Put these ingredients in the blender
and blend for 30 seconds until
smooth. Serve immediately.

· GINGER SODA ·

⅕ vanilla ice cream
⅗ ginger beer
⅕ sparkling lemonade

Whisk all the ingredients together in a blender for 45–60 seconds. Pour into a long glass and decorate with fresh mint leaves.

· GRAPEFRUIT SODA ·

⅕ vanilla ice cream
⅖ fresh grapefruit juice
⅖ sparkling water

Blend these ingredients together in a blender with a piece of cracked ice or two per person, for about 1 minute. Serve immediately in old-fashioned glasses.

· PINEAPPLE GINGER SODA ·

For each serving
⅕ vanilla or pineapple ice cream
⅕ chilled milk
⅗ ginger beer (or dry ginger ale)
5 fresh mint leaves
1 slice fresh pineapple

Blend thoroughly together in a blender for 1 minute. Serve immediately in long glasses.

• EGGNOG •

½ pint chilled milk
1 egg
½–1 oz sugar
3–4 drops vanilla essence
Grated nutmeg
Whipped cream

Beat the egg until smooth and add first the vanilla essence, then the milk stirring all the while. Strain this mixture into your serving glasses and decorate with grated nutmeg scattered over the top of whipped cream. Serves 2.

• HONEY EGGNOG •

¼ pint chilled milk
1 egg
2 tbsp honey
Nutmeg

Beat together the honey and the egg. Add the milk and beat thoroughly. Pour into an old-fashioned glass and sprinkle with powdered nutmeg.

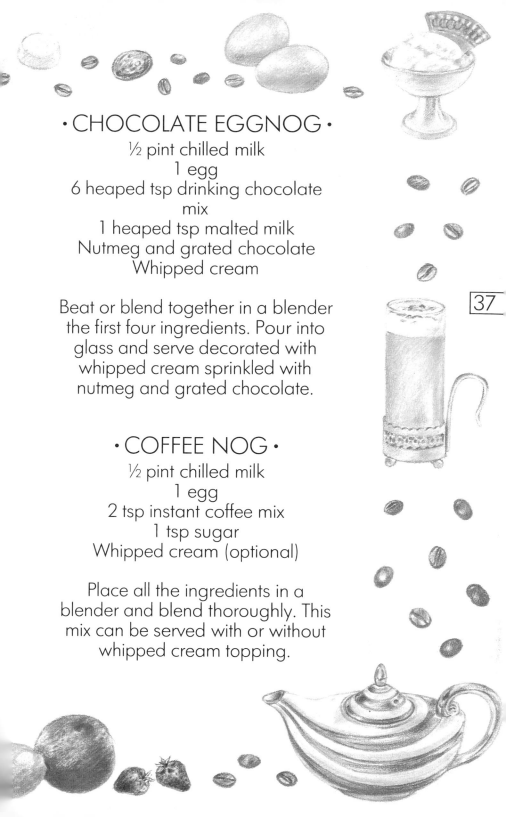

· CHOCOLATE EGGNOG ·

½ pint chilled milk
1 egg
6 heaped tsp drinking chocolate
mix
1 heaped tsp malted milk
Nutmeg and grated chocolate
Whipped cream

Beat or blend together in a blender
the first four ingredients. Pour into
glass and serve decorated with
whipped cream sprinkled with
nutmeg and grated chocolate.

· COFFEE NOG ·

½ pint chilled milk
1 egg
2 tsp instant coffee mix
1 tsp sugar
Whipped cream (optional)

Place all the ingredients in a
blender and blend thoroughly. This
mix can be served with or without
whipped cream topping.

· CHOCOLATINO ·

From the Opera Cafe on Manhattan's
West Side the most delicious coffee
concoction ever.

A double Espresso coffee
1 cup double strength drinking
chocolate
Whipped cream
Grated chocolate and grated
orange zest.

Ideally this should be served in a
hot-drink glass — that is a heavy
glass with a metal holder into
which the glass fits. If you don't
have an expresso machine use a
quarter cup very strong coffee;
pour this into the glass and stir in
the double strength chocolate. Top
this off with some whipped cream
and decorate with chocolate and
orange gratings.

· YOGURT COOLER ·

A healthy and refreshing drink from India and the Middle East, where they know about heat.

This is simply equal quantities of yogurt and water. Just blend ½ natural yogurt with ½ water, add salt and pepper to taste and serve over ice with fresh mint leaves. But there are many variations: substitute flavoured yogurts for the natural one, or use fruit juices or a mixture of fruit flesh and juice.

· YOGURT FRUIT SHAKE ·

¼ pint tub of any fruit-flavoured yogurt
½ banana
1 tsp clear honey
2 tbsp vanilla ice cream

Blend all these ingredients together in a blender until frothy. Serve immediately in a long glass. Again this recipe has variations: just experiment with different flavours of yogurt and ice cream.

· HAWAIIAN COFFEE ·

For each serving
⅓ measures of Espresso coffee
⅓ pineapple juice
⅓ coffee ice cream

Blend these ingredients together in a blender for 20–30 seconds. Pour into long chilled glasses and serve immediately.

· ICED COFFEE ·

½ pint chilled milk
2 tsp instant coffee
1 tsp sugar
4–6 drops vanilla essence
Whipping cream (optional)
Grated chocolate (optional)

Place these ingredients in a blender with cracked ice and blend for 20–30 seconds. Serve in a tall glass and decorate with whipping cream sprinkled with grated chocolate.

· ICED MINTED TEA ·

2 pints strained weak tea
1 lemon
6 stalks fresh mint
Sugar to taste

Chop the lemon and put it in the bottom of a jug, together with the chopped mint leaves and pour over the hot tea. Leave to infuse and cool for at least 30 minutes. Strain out the fruit and leaves and chill the infusion well. Serve in long glasses with lemon slice and fresh mint stalk. Serves 6–8.

· CRYSTAL CUP ·

A delicious and unusual combination

Lapsang Suchong tea
Dry ginger ale

Mix equal quantities of the cold tea and dry ginger over ice. Serve with fresh mint leaves as decoration.

· TROPICAL FRUITS ·

· PARADISE ISLAND ·

At the Lyford Cay Club this is one of the many soft, cooling drinks served to the sporty members.

¼ pineapple juice
¼ lemon juice
1 tsp grenadine
1 egg white
½ sparkling lemonade

Blend together with ice the first four ingredients for 15 seconds or so. Pour into a long glass and top up with chilled sparkling lemonade. Decorate with a slice of orange and a cherry.

· BANANA COOLER ·

For each serving simply blend together in a blender
1 banana
2 tsp instant coffee
⅔ chilled milk
⅓ chocolate ice cream
1 tsp sugar
Grated or flaked chocolate

Thoroughly blend for 15–20 seconds, serve in a tall tumbler and decorate with grated or flaked chocolate.

· SUMMER PASSION ·

⅓ passion fruit nectar
⅓ orange juice
⅙ lime juice
Dash of each of: grenadine
peppermint cordial
egg white
sugar syrup/rock candy

Shake these ingredients together well in a cocktail shaker, and serve in a highball glass over cracked ice.

· MULHERIN'S SNOW ·

Famous for her diverse and erudite knowledge on such far-flung subjects as the History of Cat Flaps and The Rivers of the World, a publisher of my long acquaintance suggests this antipodean cocktail.

⅖ passion fruit nectar
⅖ lemon sorbet
⅕ sparkling water

Throw it all in the blender with a lump of ice or two, and serve in long glasses with a straw.

· SOUTH WIND ·

⅖ pineapple juice
⅕ orange juice
⅖ single cream
Pineapple slice (optional)

Ideal for a small cocktail glass. Place these ingredients into a cocktail shaker with crushed ice and shake well. Serve in a chilled glass and decorate with a sliver of pineapple fruit.

· SUNSHINE ·

⅔ pineapple juice
⅓ lemon juice

Shake well together or blend with cracked ice. Serve in a tall glass decorated with a cherry.

· MANGOADE ·

2 ripe mangoes
2 oz sugar
Grated rind of 1 large orange
⅓ pint lime juice
⅔ pint orange juice
⅔ pint water

Combine the water, orange rind and sugar in a saucepan over heat until the sugar has dissolved. Purée the soft flesh of the mangoes in a blender and stir in the orange and lime juice. Add the syrup and the fruit mixture together and refrigerate for at least half an hour. Serve in long glasses over cracked ice. 8–10 Servings.

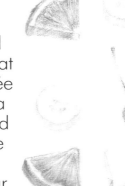

· PINEAPPLE PLUS ·

¾ pineapple juice
⅛ sugar syrup (rock candy)
Juice of ½ lemon
Pineapple slice (optional)

Mix the ingredients together
thoroughly in a cocktail shaker.
Pour over crushed ice and a sliver
of pineapple fruit.

· PINK FRUIT CUP ·
½ pineapple juice
½ orange juice
Dash of grenadine

For each person put a handful of
ice into the blender and blend the
ingredients for 10 seconds or less.
Serve in long glasses with coloured
straws.

· LIME SODA ·

For each person take
Half a banana (chopped)
⅙ lime juice
⅓ vanilla ice cream
½ sparkling water

Place all the ingredients together in a blender and blend for 30 seconds or so until smooth and frothy. Serve immediately in long glass decorated with a slice of fresh lime.

· TROPICAL SPARKLE ·

⅜ pineapple juice
⅛ lime juice
½ bitter lemon
Squeeze of lemon juice

Stir together over lots of ice in a tall glass.

·BANANA FLIP·

1 small banana
⅘ glass chilled milk
1 oz brown sugar

Place the ingredients in a blender
for 30 seconds. Serve immediately.

· PARTY PUNCHES ·

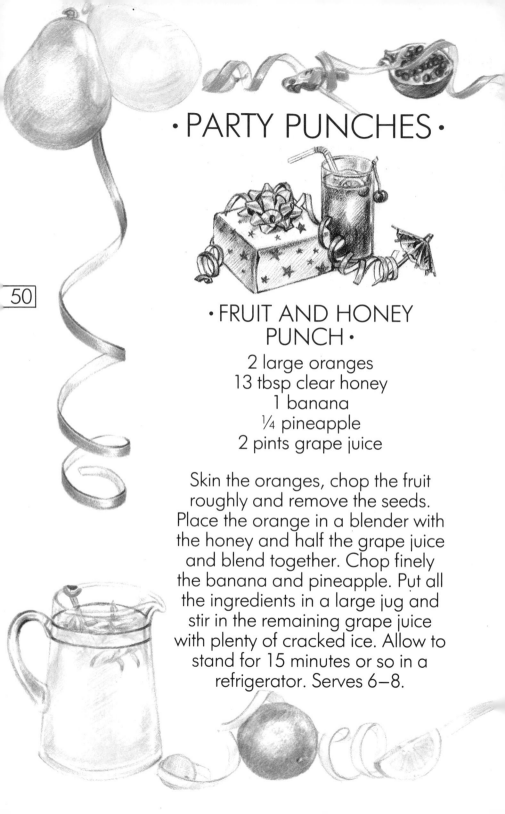

· FRUIT AND HONEY PUNCH ·

2 large oranges
13 tbsp clear honey
1 banana
¼ pineapple
2 pints grape juice

Skin the oranges, chop the fruit
roughly and remove the seeds.
Place the orange in a blender with
the honey and half the grape juice
and blend together. Chop finely
the banana and pineapple. Put all
the ingredients in a large jug and
stir in the remaining grape juice
with plenty of cracked ice. Allow to
stand for 15 minutes or so in a
refrigerator. Serves 6–8.

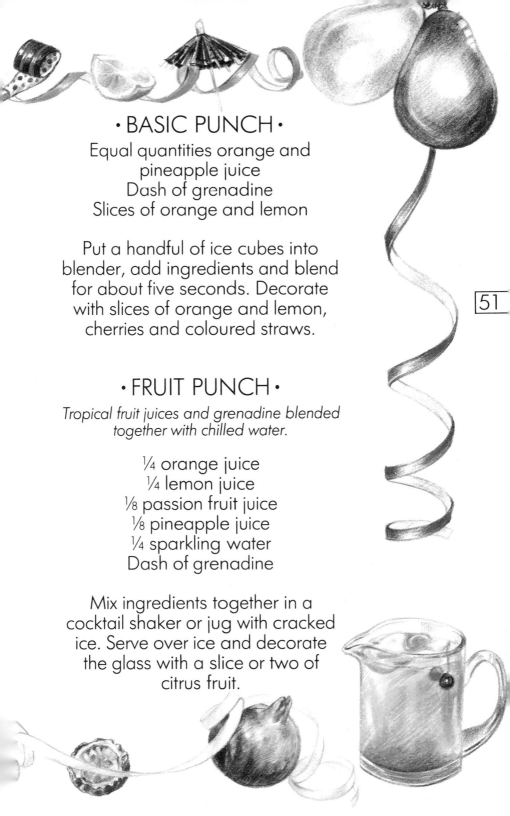

· BASIC PUNCH ·

Equal quantities orange and
pineapple juice
Dash of grenadine
Slices of orange and lemon

Put a handful of ice cubes into
blender, add ingredients and blend
for about five seconds. Decorate
with slices of orange and lemon,
cherries and coloured straws.

· FRUIT PUNCH ·

*Tropical fruit juices and grenadine blended
together with chilled water.*

¼ orange juice
¼ lemon juice
⅛ passion fruit juice
⅛ pineapple juice
¼ sparkling water
Dash of grenadine

Mix ingredients together in a
cocktail shaker or jug with cracked
ice. Serve over ice and decorate
the glass with a slice or two of
citrus fruit.

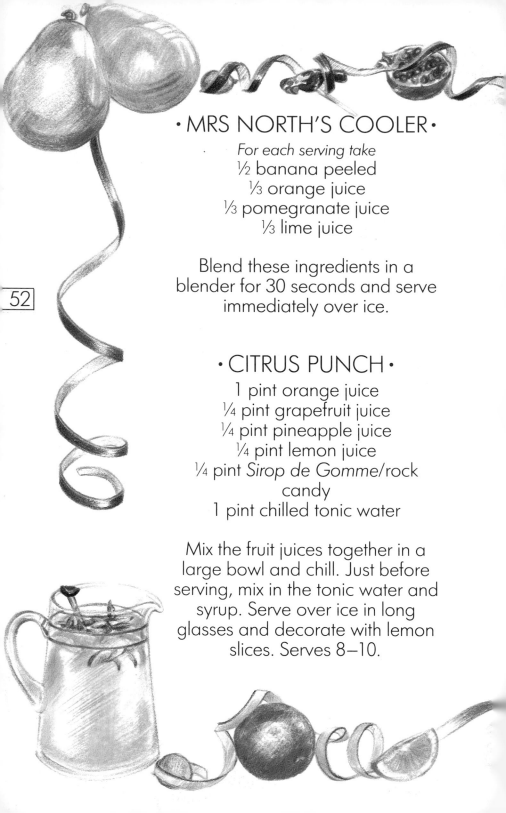

· MRS NORTH'S COOLER ·

For each serving take
½ banana peeled
⅓ orange juice
⅓ pomegranate juice
⅓ lime juice

Blend these ingredients in a
blender for 30 seconds and serve
immediately over ice.

· CITRUS PUNCH ·

1 pint orange juice
¼ pint grapefruit juice
¼ pint pineapple juice
¼ pint lemon juice
¼ pint *Sirop de Gomme*/rock
candy
1 pint chilled tonic water

Mix the fruit juices together in a
large bowl and chill. Just before
serving, mix in the tonic water and
syrup. Serve over ice in long
glasses and decorate with lemon
slices. Serves 8–10.

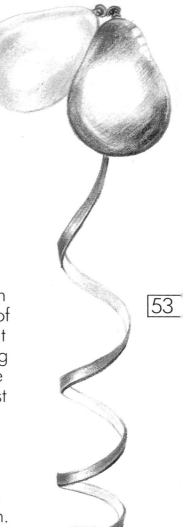

· SUMMER FIZZ ·

12 stalks of fresh mint
½ pint water
¼ pint redcurrant jelly
Juice of 1 lemon
2 pints ginger beer
⅔ pint orange juice

Crush the mint stalks and leaves in
a bowl with a mortar or the back of
a large spoon. Add the redcurrant
jelly and half of the water at boiling
temperature. Stir together until the
jelly is dissolved, then stir in the rest
of the water cold. Leave to cool
and then strain off the mint and
discard it. Add the fruit juice and
chill. Stir in the ginger beer just
before serving, and pour over ice
and use fresh mint as a decoration.
Serves 8–10.

53

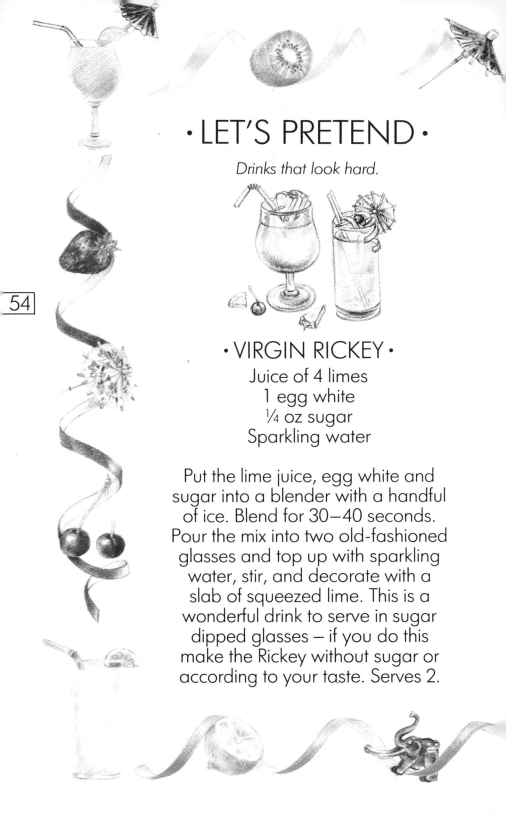

· LET'S PRETEND ·

Drinks that look hard.

· VIRGIN RICKEY ·

Juice of 4 limes
1 egg white
¼ oz sugar
Sparkling water

Put the lime juice, egg white and sugar into a blender with a handful of ice. Blend for 30–40 seconds. Pour the mix into two old-fashioned glasses and top up with sparkling water, stir, and decorate with a slab of squeezed lime. This is a wonderful drink to serve in sugar dipped glasses – if you do this make the Rickey without sugar or according to your taste. Serves 2.

· TAME COLLINS ·

Everything except the gin.

Juice of 1 lemon
Sparkling water
Sugar

Take the juice from the lemon and
add sugar to taste. Shake or stir
over cracked ice and strain into a
tall glass. Add more ice and top up
the glass with chilled sparkling
water. Decorate with lemon zest, a
slice of orange and a cherry
threaded onto an umbrella. Serve
with a straw.

· VIRGIN COLADA ·

Everything but the rum.

⅕ coconut cream
⅘ pineapple juice
Pineapple slivers

Mix the coconut cream and
pineapple juice together in a
shaker or blender. Pour over
cracked ice in a long tumbler and
decorate with fruit.

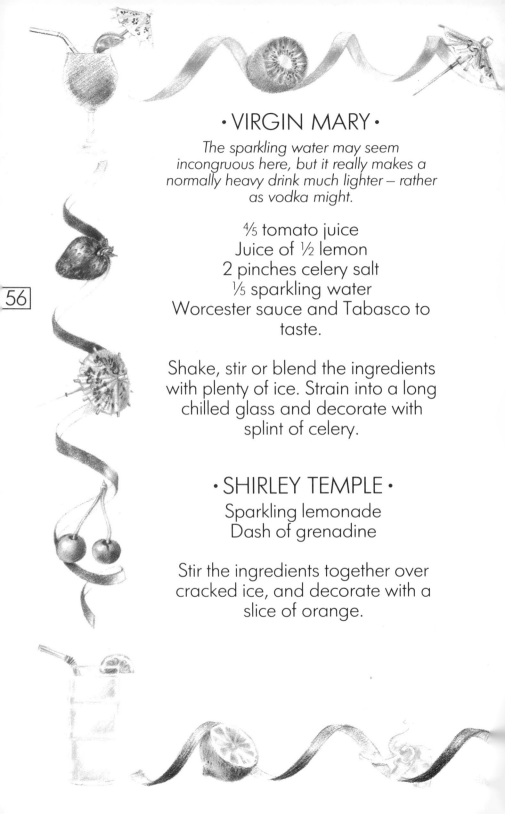

· VIRGIN MARY ·

*The sparkling water may seem
incongruous here, but it really makes a
normally heavy drink much lighter – rather
as vodka might.*

⅘ tomato juice
Juice of ½ lemon
2 pinches celery salt
⅕ sparkling water
Worcester sauce and Tabasco to
taste.

Shake, stir or blend the ingredients
with plenty of ice. Strain into a long
chilled glass and decorate with
splint of celery.

· SHIRLEY TEMPLE ·

Sparkling lemonade
Dash of grenadine

Stir the ingredients together over
cracked ice, and decorate with a
slice of orange.

· STAY SOBER ·

⅛ grenadine
⅛ lemon syrup
⁶⁄₈ tonic water

Stir the ingredients together over
cracked ice in a long glass.

· FRENCH TEASE ·

*From the French House in Soho, the first
suggestion for a soft drink was white wine
and soda – but this mixture can make
'grown' men feel uncomfortable, due to its
amazing hue.*

Orange juice
Grenadine

Stir some orange juice over plenty
of ice adding grenadine in liberal
quantity until the colour really
appeals to you. You can substitute
grapefruit juice for the orange if
you prefer a slightly sharper drink –
it requires less grenadine too.

· SOUR VIRGIN ·

Juice of 2 fresh lemons
Sugar to taste
Sparkling water
1 or 2 drops green food colouring
(optional)

Put the lemon juice, colouring and
sugar into a blender and blend
with ice for 15–20 seconds. Pour
this into chilled highball glass and
top up with sparkling water to
taste. Decorate with a slice of
lemon and a cherry.

· BULLOCK SHOT ·

*Most softened drinks seem to be feminine
to judge from the number of virgins – here
is an emasculated if singular male:*

¼ pint beef bouillon (canned)
Juice of ½ lemon
Worcester sauce and Tabasco to
taste.

Put the ingredients in a cocktail
shaker with plenty of ice. Shake
thoroughly and serve 'straight-up'
in a cocktail glass.

· LONG BOAT FIZZ ·

¼ lime juice
¾ ginger beer
Fresh mint

Stir the ingredients together in a
long tumbler over lots of ice.
Decorate with fresh mint stalks.

· INDEX OF RECIPES ·

· INDEX OF INGREDIENTS ·

61

Citrus Punch 52
Grapefruit Soda 34
Grapes
  Fruit and Honey Punch 50
  Grape Delight 24
  Grape Rickey 25
Grenadine
  Basic Punch 51
  Driver's Dream 12
  French Tease 57
  Fruit Punch 51
  Paradise Island 42
  Parson's Dose 20
  Pink Fruit Cup 47
  Pussy Foot 16
  Savoy Sportsman 15
  Shirley Temple 56
  Sportsman 18
  Stay Sober 57
  Summer Passion 43

Honey
  Fruit and Honey Punch 50
  Honey Eggnog 36
  Lemon Aperitif 16
  Yogurt Fruit Shake 39

Ice cream, Chocolate
  Banana Cooler 43
  Chocolate Malted Milk 30
  Vienna Velvet 29
Ice cream, Coffee
  Hawaiian Coffee 40
Ice cream, Pineapple
  Pineapple Ginger Soda 35
Ice cream, Strawberry
  Strawberry Malted Milk 31
Ice cream, Vanilla
  Banana Milkshake 32
  Chocolate Mint 28
  Ginger Soda 34
  Grapefruit Soda 34
  Lime Soda 48
  Orange Milkshake 33
  Pineapple Ginger Soda 35
  Strawberry Milkshake 33
  Vanilla Malted 31

Vanilla Milkshake 32
Yogurt Fruit Shake 39

Lemons, Lemon juice
  Bullock Shot 59
  Cinderella 11
  Citrus Bliss 10
  Citrus Punch 52
  Driver's Dream 12
  Fruit Punch 51
  Ginger Peach 14
  Grape Delight 24
  Iced Minted Tea 41
  Lemon Aperitif 16
  Paradise Island 42
  Pineapple Plus 46
  Preston's Potion 17
  Pussy Foot 16
  Raspberry and Lemonade 18
  Raspberry Lemon Cocktail 27
  Raspberry Refresher 26
  Real Lemon Barley Water 21
  Real Lemonade 13
  Real Tomato Juice 22
  Savoy Sportsman 15
  Sour Virgin 58
  Sportsman 18
  Stay Sober 57
  Summer Fizz 53
  Sunshine 45
  Tame Collins 55
  Very Bitter Lemon 19
  Virgin Mary 56
Lemon, Bitter
  Tropical Sparkle 48
Lemon sorbet
  Mulherin's Snow 44
Lemonade, Sparkling
  Ginger Soda 34
  Paradise Island 42
  Saint Clement's 18
  Shirley Temple 56
Limes
  Citrus Bliss 10
  Grape Rickey 25
  Lemon Aperitif 16

Lime Soda 48
Long Boat Fizz 59
Mangoade 45
Minted Orange 11
Mrs North's Cooler 52
Pussy Foot 16
Savoy Sportsman 15
Summer Passion 43
Thirst Aid 19
Tropical Sparkle 48
Virgin Rickey 54

Malted milk
  Chocolate Eggnog 37
  Chocolate Malted Milk 30
  Strawberry Malted Milk 31
  Vanilla Malted 31
Mangoes
  Mangoade 45
Milk
  Banana Cooler 43
  Banana Flip 49
  Banana Milkshake 32
  Chocolate Malted Milk 30
  Chocolate Mint 28
  Eggnogs 36–7
  Iced Coffee 40
  Peppermint Chocolate Cream 29
  Pineapple Ginger Soda 35
  Strawberry Malted Milk 31
  Vanilla Malted 31
  Vanilla Milkshake 32
Milk, Dry, skimmed
  Orange Milkshake 33
Mint
  Iced Minted Tea 41
  Long Boat Fizz 59
  Minted Orange 11
  Pineapple Ginger Soda 35
  Summer Fizz 53
  Tomato and Orange Cocktail 25

Nectarines
  Chocolate Malted Milk 30

Oranges, Orange Juice
  Basic Punch 51

Cinderella 11
Citrus Bliss 10
Citrus Punch 52
French Tease 57
Fruit and Honey Punch 50
Fruit Punch 51
Ginger Peach 14
Mangoade 45
Minted Orange 11
Mrs North's Cooler 52
Orange Milkshake 33
Parson's Dose 20
Peach and Orange Cocktail 13
Pink Fruit Cup 47
Pussy Foot 16
Saint Clement's 17
South Wind 44
Sportsman 18
Summer Fizz 53
Summer Passion 43
Tomato and Orange Cocktail 25

Parsnips
  Parsnip Surprise 26
Passion fruit
  Fruit Punch 51
  Mulherin's Snow 44
  Summer Passion 43
Peaches
  Ginger Peach 14
  Peach and Orange Cocktail 13
Peppermint
  Chocolate Mint 28
  Peppermint Chocolate Cream 29
  Summer Passion 43
Pineapple
  Basic Punch 51
  Cinderella 11
  Citrus Punch 52
  Driver's Dream 12
  Fruit and Honey Punch 50
  Fruit Punch 51
  Hawaiian Coffee 40
  Paradise Island 42
  Parsnip Surprise 26
  Pineapple Ginger Soda 35